Poetic Tributes
to
My Family
GROWING IN FAITH

Norma Jean Thigpen

Published by Passion Publications
A division of Tell The Truth International
7005 Woodbine Ave
Sacramento, Ca. 95822
tellthetruthsac@gmail.com

Printed in the United States of America
Copyright ©2024

Cover image and design by:
Charlyn_designs

ISBN: 978-1-957101-05-7

This book of poetry is dedicated to my
Dear Mother and Father, Christine Keys Thigpen
and Joseph Thigpen.

My mother was a survivor and child of God
who loved the Creator with all her heart.
She continues to be an inspiration to her children
who recall the beautiful interactions with her.

Special mention is also given to Dr. Robert and
Mary Fairley, longtime friends and mentors.
And a special thanks to Donald G. Adams who
encouraged me to publish my poems.

CONTENTS

FOREWORD

Unconditional Love
Reverence to God, Loyalty and Humility

Norma was born on January 8, on the day she came home from the hospital, my mother would learn that there was no heat in the house. Most likely our dad had gambled, been rolled or drank the money away that should have been used to buy coal. My mother recounted this story to us when we were older. If you have ever been to Northeast Ohio in the winter, you know it gets very cold.

Knowing Norma, I bet that she didn't even cry. She would never let her discomfort cause anyone concern. My mother likely huddled us around the fireplace. Sitting by the fireplace is something we both enjoy to this day. We were shaped not to complain and like many children of our era we were conditioned to be seen and not heard. Perhaps that is what inspired Norma to take up her pen and express her inner thoughts becoming a poetess.

Our mother, the chef, grandfathered in because of her talent, could cook anything from lobster thermador to the most delectable prime rib. On Thursday nights, she made her beef tips over noodles and many local mafia members would come into the restaurant for it. Many times, they would personally come to the kitchen to give her a big tip in her hands. I tell you these things about my mother because the fruit doesn't fall far from the tree.

Back to poetess…meek, gentle, congenial, kind, patient, long suffering are very good adjectives to describe her but a Humble Servant is Best. She loves the Lord with all her soul, heart and being. I have seen her refuse to assert her rights when she has been misjudged or wronged.

The assault rolls away like water off a duck's back. She has adopted the Keys women's philosophy using the arsenal available in prayer, seeking the Savior's face prostrate and surrendered. This is an example of that meekness, control under pressure. Somehow, she remains poised when I am fuming and about to explode over a situation.

You see, she has learned Jeremiah 29:11, for whatever God has planned for you cannot be thwarted. His plan that I see is her living submitted to God and living by faith. She lives John 13:34, "A new command I give you, love one another as I have loved you, so you must love one another."

As I consider her life, I do believe in due season, God will reward her double for her trouble in this earthly walk as He did Job. But more importantly, her acts of selflessness, steadfast and devotion to the Master will earn her the "Crown of Life." As I close, I would like to share a plaque that I gave her: "Sisters by Birth but Friends by Choice".

For God be the Glory for the Great works that He has done in and through her.

Dr. Jereline Kendrick

FROM THE AUTHOR

I began journaling as a small child and continued through adulthood. I have selected some of those writings for this book. This is a collection of experiences with people I have met from childhood through today. Throughout my life, I have encountered and/or been in the presence of people who loved God. Those experiences have shaped my outlook on life and made me the person I am today.

My poems and prose are written from the heart and given to you with love. I pray that these writings will give you peace, joy, laughter, and tears as you recount the memories of our loved ones and others who you don't know but may understand their story as well.

More than 20 years ago, at St. John Missionary Baptist Church under Dr. Robert Fairley, I fell in love with Jesus and was <u>thirsty</u> for his Word. I love the Lord with all my heart; He is my Savior and Lord. I believe that nothing is impossible for God. May my words on these pages give hope and smiles to those who know what it means to grow in faith.

Joseph Thigpen
(My Father)

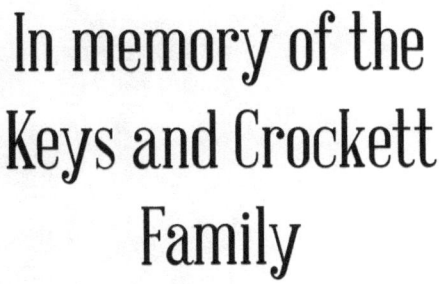

In memory of the Keys and Crockett Family

Christine L. Thigpen
(My Mother)

CHRISTINE

C is for the Christian woman

H is for Honor to God

R is for Respecting the process

I is for Imagining the possibilities

S is for her beautiful Smile

T is for Timely advice

I is for Ironing out the differences

N is for Never giving up

E is for Eternal rest with the Savior

Love to you!

Eugene and Harriet Keys
Christine's Parents

MOMMA'S COAT

Momma's coat has seen some days,
The coat may look old
With all the buttons clinging
To a string so thin
And long with wear

Momma's coat has seen some days,
The depression is evident in its appearance
First Grandma had it
It was appreciated when Grandpa
Bought it for Christmas

Momma's coat has seen some days
Grandma used it as her "Sunday go the meeting" coat
She used it and prized it
Then passed it down the line

Momma's coat has seen some days
As the buttons are resewn,
The smile on Momma's face is reassuring.
She is quite proud to wear it
As she goes to work and the PTA

Momma's coat has seen some days
It has been around at least fifty years
The stories it could tell…
Yet Momma's coat is still around
And I can't wait until it is mine.

Top: Louise, Jolivia, Ann, Louise
Bottom: Christa, ChayLa, Chynna (Christine's great
grandchildren and Mary Louise Hudson's grandchildren)

LOUISE

L is for her Love for her daughters and grandchildren

O is for Thinking outside the box

U is for Utilizing her resources

I is for Imaging the possibilities

S is for Seeking the truth always

E is for knowing Everything will be alright

Top left: Arlene Thigpen and Reginald J
Top right: Reginald J. Thigpen and Reginald Jr
Bottom: Jereline, Louise, Christa, Clarence, LaTrese, Arlene

ARLENE

A is for her Amazing personality

R is for her Respect for the person's feelings

L is for the Agape love she has for all people

E is for her Everlasting faith in God

N is for her Nice and Generous heart

E is for Everlasting hope of finding the truth

Top: Annie Mae and Uncle Jewel
Siblings: Betty Williams, Charles Keys,
Carolyn Keys and Luvenia Love
Christine Thigpen's siblings
Bottom: James Keys

CAROLYN SMILES

(In Memory of Carolyn Keys)

Ever wonder how Christians
are to be converted and become as little children?
Carolyn exemplifies that demeanor to us.

Often she speaks in childlike phrases,
Giggling like a young school girl;
Jesus expects us to keep the behavior of children while
carrying out the responsibilities of adulthood.

Who can find a righteous woman?
One who has genuine childlike love for family,
her children, grandchildren and friends?
She cares for her mother and siblings
while she was young,

She did every measure of servant hood in her
youth and that warrants a crown of glory.
She is full of joy-the joy described in Galatians.

Her laughter is contagious as she
remembers her childhood.
Her loving hand is upon her children;
She seeks to provide for their needs;

She retreats to her new place,
a heavenly place where she can be served.
She retreats to her God who is provider of all;

And finally she retreats to her mother,
father, siblings and she cries.
At last, she smiles and giggles as God says,
"Good and Faithful Servant, Well Done!"

There are crowns and rewards for those called by
God who carries out the orders of servanthood.
2 Timothy 4:8 states,
"There is a crown laid up for me, the crown
of righteousness which the Lord,
the righteous judge will give on that Day.
This crown is for all who believe in Jesus, the Christ.

**Top: Eugene Keys Jr in the military
(sibling to Christine Thigpen)
Below: Eugene Keys and his son, Curtis Keys**

MY UNCLE BOY

On a Life Well-Lived
(In Memory of Eugene Keys)

Uncle Boy is a soldier
Believing in God
Always keeping the peace
Father to his children
Actively loving his sons
Nurturer to his nieces and nephews

A man in solemn mediation
Always erect, quiet and resolute
One with deep contemplation
Always a soldier walking with pride

Watching but not participating
One can only imagine
The pain or sorrow
That lives in the soul
As one reflects on the lives of others

A man of many talents
A good cook
A great gardener
The handy man's gift
A plumber of sorts
A great provider
Loving through action
Fond reflections
Good wishes
Hearty laughter
A great smile

Top: Lloyd R. Keys (Sonny)
Bottom: Louise and Sonny as kids

GRATITUDE

(In Memory of Sonny)

Jesus touched my life one day
When I had no sense of play
When I was burdened low in sin
And could not find my way

Jesus touched my life one day
He gave me a sense of play
He said don't forget
you are here to smile
And help others find their way

Jesus touched my life one day
And He washed my sins away
I took a breath
I was submerged
And I began to see the way

Jesus touched my life one day
With His merciful Hand
He taught me how to pray
He took my sins
shed them away
And set me on my way

Donte, Sylvia, Danielle, and Jessie

SWEET REST...

(In Memory of Donte)

To know Donte is to LOVE Donte
Smiling, jesting and jiving, taking everything light
On surface appearance cruising day and night
Listening, thinking, rocking, and rolling

Momma's voice was always calling
With words of wisdom
As a young man school is important
Essentially a child prodigy pegged to succeed

Traveled the country with Momma and Danielle
California, to Mississippi, to
Colorado, Chicago and more
As an adult he was so proud of those journeys
But a crush and opportunity lead him back to Chicago

So much fun and parties at night
He's so congenial and taught not to fight
Landed a big job in the City
Houston's where he settled for his life
Computer whiz, networking guru, pretty woman
A serious commitment...

A few years of career focus
Uncle Charles, Junior, and Jereline
and so many in his life
Many didn't see him and will think he never lived
But so evasive was he
It seemed life was too short
He didn't have time to appreciate the good things

A gentle soul still sorry for his shortcomings as a child
A child prodigy, a genius and good hearted young man
Life is what we give it and take for ourselves

God is the Creator and the Giver of life
God sets the numbers and we use the time
Yes, it was too short in our eyes
but it was the life he lived.
His experiences and opportunities
outnumbered his short life.

We pray that God gives the family rest and peace.

PRECIOUS TRACEY LOVE

Psalm 116:15
(In her memory)

There is special consideration for Harriet Love
known as Tracey
"Why?" you ask.
She has the demeanor of her grandmother,
for whom she was named.

I would assume her humility was inherited
Because she is the close image of her grandmother
in stature and disposition
Just, like Harriet, Tracey prepares delicious
southern dishes for her family
She always prepared meals for her children

Tracey is well educated and she is computer literate
Because of her humility and silence
Many family members don't see her true value
and discount her worth

She would surprise you greatly
She is a nurse by trade and is the mother
of four young men and one daughter
Tracey understands but is careful to
withhold and not speak her mind
Many of the young men and women
would benefit from her knowledge
When she was young, she took the responsibility
of caring for her mother

Tracey made sacrifices for her mother
so her mother could live a good life
Through it all, Tracey did not complain

God is pleased at how she cared for her mother
God is pleased with how she nurtured her children
God forgives all shortcomings if you call on His
name and Believe that Jesus is the Christ

God is our portion this
God knows all and is able to do all things
In her silence, I believe Tracey knew it all and
God's grace provided comfort
So precious in the sight of the Lord
is the death of his saints

Top: Norma and Aunt Luvenia
Below: Zaria Love and grandmother Luvenia love

A SOLDIER GONE HOME

(A Tribute to Luvenia Love)

During my early years
God was in the distance
A God of the Israelites
A God of my resistance

There were obstacles to my faith
Many good times were in the way
School and parties were such a heavy weight
But He gave me a truth and a plan not to stray

Without delay God gave me a family
Children, grand and great grand children
My life was settling down
God was getting near

I praised and worshipped His name
I paid my offering and tithes
Worship was becoming the best game
I was in church all the time

Then God stepped in and steadied my pace
He put a light in my heart
God gave me the strength to run the race

My praises were sincere
My paths were made straight
My calling was clear

Finally, I saw Him in full attire
He is a God to be revered
He is the only one that I can admire

He is the one and only living God
The Alpha and the Omega
The Great Savior of the universe
My God and My Creator

As I rest, I know many won't understand my life's calling
And the God who ordained it
My calling was to be bold in my approach
My boldness may have offended some
But if I drew you to Christ, there are no apologies
Many may not ever know Him

I leave to my clan
My children and my friends
My love for God and His Son Jesus
Christ as the only saving plan

It is only in Christ that we truly live
Please forgive my mistakes
Only God can sustain and revive
Remember me as a child of God
and now present in His Arms

Tributes

Top: Late Dr. Robert Leonard Fairley
Left and Bottom: with his wife Mary Fairley and others

FAIRLEY...THE MAN

(Dedicated to Pastor Robert Leonard Fairley)

It is good to have a friend
In a man who is true
To both his immediate family
And church folk like you.

And one can only attribute
His genuine love and kindness
To the Master high in the sky,
To the Mighty force,
That directs him by and by.

And who am I to write
This poem about this man of God
Only, one of many worshippers
Who has benefited from his love

He sits down with the mourners
On the mourner's bench;
He brings the word of comfort
That God freely sent.

And through his gentle ministering
Those quiet whispered words
Or precious hug or kiss
He shares, confirms he is Spirit led.

In just ten years
Goals and missions were affirmed
In just ten years
St. John has grown and learned-

The church is not the building
Nor the fancy clothes we wear;
The church is the peace of Christ
We carry on our busy way.

Quietly through example
He taught us to go out
Not to late night clubs
But to the streets as beacon lights

And it can be said of Mary
That she will never be far from his side
Like Coretta to Martin,
She shines bright as a star.

And as this poem concludes,
It does not conclude the Love
That each St. John member carries
In their hearts for him
Given from God above

MARGARET

A Christian Sister at St. John in East Palo Alto, Ca.

Merry is the one who seeks God

Angelic is the voice who sing praises

Reverent is the spirit in worship

Godly is the man who keeps peace

Armor is the protection for battle

Righteous is the one who obeys

Eternal is the life that Jesus gives

Trustworthy is the one who abides in God

Dedications

Top: Jereline receiving diploma
Middle left: Jereline speaking
Bottom: Robert B. Kendrick (her son)
graduating the 8th grade and Jereline

SISTERS ARE
FOREVER FRIENDS

(Dedicated to Jereline)

Great sisters are to be shared
Thoughtful sisters become best friends
Exceptional sisters achieve phenomenal success
Healing Sisters understand there are hearts to mend

It was just yesterday and Jereline was a child
Always making plans, working and saving for the future
As a teen she carefully saved to buy Christmas gifts
Often selling small personal items
to make a nickel or dime

In high school giving came in the form of the Tri-Hi-Y
Honor's Club, Candy Stripper at the hospital
In college, in the form of gifts and even a family car

She always had time for family,
friends and colleagues
Her husband and son depend on her
for keeping things balanced

At work, everyone feels her love and maternal nature
She bakes cookies and cakes to break the ice
And lend a quiet ear as everyone talks, so nice
With Jereline, nothing is impossible
no matter what stage of life she's in
All things are possible if you keep God within

With her constant dreaming
She was blessed with a husband and friend
Along came her son named Barack
The Mother of Whom He would depend

Through her thoughtful acts
She'd find time to travel
Italy, France, Fiji, Africa, Angola and much more
Often sharing the details of her travels
Understanding the importance
of every person she meets

Quietly, through her faith
she helped others to cope
Through her loving ministry
she helped others to find hope

Her gift is her ministry
Her ministry is her occupation
Her help comes through
her God-given wisdom

Shirley Gunther, daughter of Betty Williams

COUSINS LIKE SISTERS

Shirley Gunther
(Happy 70th Birthday)

Shirley is one of our favorite cousins
She is fondly called Pretty Mama by her grandchildren
But many people call her sister and friend.
She has a smile as big as life
She has a heart of pure gold
She spends her time defying strife
There is no problem that she can't mend.

She has intuition and insight
She has love and compassion
She exhibits the qualities of Christ
Throughout the day and night

We are not surprised by these accolades
She comes from the Keys-Crockett line
She comes from a line of royalty not renegades
Her grandparents are Eugene and Harriet Keys

Her mother is Betty Williams
Her first years of life were spent in Mississippi
In Mississippi, the country life was good
Fresh fruits and vegetables
Fresh hog and beef smoked with wood

Clothes although few were clean and pressed
Shirley literally lived as a queen.
From humble beginnings to a life full with Christ
She plans her days in service to the King
She doesn't have to worry because He paid the price

Anderson Jones: at far left with cousins

HOW COUSINS BEHAVE

Anderson Jones

Words don't come easy as I remember my cousin
Even though we hadn't spoken for years
But at one time we all lived in Youngstown
And there lingers a fondness for one so dear

Betty was the next in line of the sisters
The family that lived on the Northside
Christine was the eldest daughter
The family that lived on the Southside

They were children who migrated from Brookhaven
Spreading their wings for a better life
Yet remembering the training
learned from the south

Willie (Abdul), Shirley, Louise, Lloyd,
Celester (Brother), Diane, Jereline,
Anderson (Bubble), Norma, and Arlene

Anderson grew up in Youngstown
A city in Northeast Ohio
A city filled with an uptown and downtown
Filled with Srouss, Woolworth and movie theaters
Frequented by children, cousins on the weekends

Every other weekend first cousins met at the cinema
So much intrigue and wonder seen by each one
A city full of life and great adventure was done
On weekends the cousins spent time together
Cousins had fun and had sleepovers
Laughing and playing throughout the night
It didn't matter to them what the weather
It seemed good times would last forever.

As they grew up and the childhood times came to an end
They began to work and some to college
Others went off to military service
They returned to visit their mothers
But they all obtained knowledge

Anderson was always the cunning the quiet son
Living life calmly and without strife
He set to his work and started his life
In Texas no doubt and he married a wife

Erica and her children were around
Still Diane and Shirley continued to be bound
To the faith of their mother Betty Jean
But always looking back to the times spent as kids.
Remembering their cousins
and their Youngstown daydreams

Jereline, Norma, and Arlene

SISTER, SISTER
DREAM DREAMS

Sister, Sister
I see a reflection in the mirror of my sisters,
Progeny coming after me,
I see hope, and the dreams that I seek.
I see the sun and the moon shining on the streets
I see the hope that was lost some time ago
Being revived in their eyes—
beautiful, prettier than mine

All anew, the dreams I had stopped dreaming
All anew the songs that I had stopped singing
Coming to life in the young women of the future
I see my sisters,
Progeny, coming after me,
A renewal of strength,
A healthy breed

Sisters who love themselves,
Clothed in expensive robes,
Powerful—the best they can be
With smiles on their faces
And the hope in brothers standing on the streets
Dreaming dreams like beautiful African women
Sister sister, Dream dreams

SUNNY SUN

(Dedicated to Sunny Azah)

The Sun because of its greatness
shines through a forest;
illuminating every inch
of space it comes into.

It does not stop for the hare
That hides near a bush
Hoping to confuse its predator
Nor the caterpillar that
Pecks and pecks its cocoon.

To emerge a butterfly
Nor the lonely child covering her face
in hope of finding peace
The sunny sun brings great joy
Strengthens and encourages
for a renewed life.
It is love.

DEDICATED TO MRS. ELLEN H. ANDERSON

Her life was a whisper of
what it could have been
Her voice was a sweet melody
of all life had been to her
Her kindness was like a fresh bouquet
that only God can send.
Her legacy is her smile in adversity
and her belief in God
whom she called upon so often

A PICTURE OF THE HEART

(Dedicated to Dr. Rosita Saw)
Manager at Santa Clara County, California

As we look into the camera
May our eyes only see the good
That each woman can offer all humankind
In the course of work and play

As we frame the picture
Look for the compassionate soothing nature
One that touches very few
In the course of many generations

As we open the shutter
Look for the one
who can smile in adversity
And offer hope in despair
And help lift the burdens
We carry from day to day

As we close the shutter
May our eyes only see the good
That each person can offer all humankind
In the course of work and play

A SIMPLE POEM FOR A SOPHISTICATED LADY

(Dedicated to Ms. Audrey Simmons)

Professionally, there will be a void
No one will be able to fill the shoes
In fact no one will ever impact
The lives of young people
As she has done throughout the years
Even when the position is filled!

Culturally, we will be deprived in the workplace,
Of a professional connoisseur who
understands the subtleness of Bach
to the Afghani traditions in the Mediterranean
We will miss a jewel, a precious stone
Always willing to share her experiences

Personally, there will be a loss of a mentor
in the workplace,
One who empowers, encourages
And befriends those who are willing to disagree
When everyone else says you are the greatest
For only a friend sees the tired eyes
And the mental stress and strain

Professionally, there will be a void
No one will be able to fill her shoes
No one will impact the lives of those teens
As she has done throughout the years
Even when the position is filled!

PASTORS ARE GODS INSTRUMENTS

Happy Pastor's Anniversary
(Dedicated to Pastor Ellis)

From Paul Tillich to Eric Fromm
Pastor Ellis is well versed
On the I am of being
To the various forms of Love

From Another Country by Baldwin
To I know why the caged bird sings
by Angelou

Pastor Ellis is sensitive
to the needs of the race
And the specific concerns
of the church

From Abrams to Abraham
From Jacob to Israel
Pastor Ellis is cognizant
Of the subtleties of God
As He changes a name

From a colleague to a friend
From a student to a mentor
Pastor Ellis has learned
Ministers need encouragement
Ministers need friends

From an acquaintance to a friend
From a friend to a wife
Pastor Ellis knows only God
Can grow the seeds
Of the marriage he has with Van

From a church body called Pilgrim
From most gracious saints of God
From singles especially
To the Pastor whom they love

To his wife they hold dearly
To our Precious Lord and Savior
They say boldly, Reverend Ellis
We love and support you

PRAISES IN THE STORM

(Dedication to Thurman Washington)

In the stillness of my room
lying across my bed
Visions of lifelong service
appear in my head

Ask firm for forgiveness
and make a new pledge
To the cross at Calvary
to God the Mighty Edge.

When the storms are raging
and the masses cannot rest
A joyful soul finds comfort
in Christ who is the best

Moving in Abraham's bosom
sweet Lazarus can relate
There is no greater peace
than the peace found in faith

But can faith birth the refuge
that is needed to survive?
Can Jesus provide the comfort
in which each soul can hide?
Just as John received the blessing
when Jesus was submerged
All received the comfort
as the blood emerged

Does the Master continue to bless
in the raging storm?
Is there solace
when the saints don't conform?

For a blessing is a blessing
when atoned with Jesus' blood
But first bow down in prayer,
blessings He will flood

Through all we must praise Him
in a foreign place
Fill sorrowful hearts with joy
when we can't plead our case

Take the martyr stance
along with His precious Hand
Lead minds to glory
and glory we can demand

-THROUGH HER PRAYER

(Dedicated to Barbara McNeal)

There is nothing more precious
than a saint
Who knows the Lord.

The eagerness in her voice
The silent reverent disposition
That shows through adversity
And overflows with joy

It is not the years spent in service
Nor the number of services that we attend
It is the positive answer to the question
Did you feed my sheep my friend?

Most diligently
Barbara served Him in her stead
And if you hadn't met Him
You would have seen Him
in her prayer

Poetry in Motion

TODAY

Today was the most beautiful day
The shining sun,
the beautiful smiling faces
And the peaceful wind
left a happy feeling in my heart

I want to sing and dance,
Then lie around a campfire all night
But I suppressed the feelings
and did my everyday chores.

COLLEGE

The first day is always fun
The first day no work is done
The first day everyone's your chum
But this is the second and I'm not dumb

ALLEGIANCE

I pledge allegiance to myself
and not to a forsaken flag
I pledge allegiance to myself
And to all who pledge to themselves

SLAVERY

My parents were dragged
To a white foreign country
Leaving their previous cultures

IMPLICATIONS OF LOVE

An occasional wink says he is looking
A roving hand means watch out, he's fresh
A proposition means you are flirting too
A date means you are worth being seem with
A total rejection means you blew it

WHEN EVERYTHING'S RIGHT

I enjoy a good laugh
When everything is right!
I can appreciate a good time
When everything is right!
I even rebel against society
When everything is right!

FIRST TRUE LOVE

I do not know what true love is
Once I was told that I was blessed with it
It would supply its own meaning
I do not know the proper age for a love
Once I was told that my love would be older
He is supposed to be older
I am not sure if I have been socialized
Or if I was told the truth on the matter
Because I am falling for someone younger
And my falling is faster than any other love
Does that sound like true love?
Would I be writing this corny poem?

EMOTIONS

Many people live in houses,
which are roughly built.
But I live in a home
That will never tilt.

THE TRAIN

Ten minutes
A man running
Eight minutes
Three blocks
Six minutes
South Pacific Depot
Four minutes
Engines roaring
Two minutes
Porter closing
Zero minutes
Training leaving

INNER PEACE

To sing songs
no one understands
To say things
and everyone stares

To dream
when everyone worries
To love
when hate has filled the air

To smile
when the rebel takes the stand
To cry
when the surprise was pleasing
To talk
when everyone is silent
To live
when everyone is dead.

LAW-ABIDING

When the amendment
was made for voting,
I wasn't included
but I didn't fight.

I am law abiding
When the Internal Revenue said,
I must pay taxes
I surrendered easily, I didn't fight

I am law abiding
When the President said go to war
I went to war. I did fight
I died too!
I am law abiding

SMILES

One thousand muscles
One memory
Of a hot summer day
One hundred wrinkles
One memory
Of the picnic basket
One man
One woman
One small daffodil
Of the green pasture makes
One thousand muscles
One hundred wrinkles
A smile